THE ART OF WAR

OF BERNADOTTE

as elucidated from the

Resumé of Military Principles by

Carl XV of Sweden, Bernadotte's grandson

translated and somewhat abridged by

DANIEL I. RADAKOVICH

NIMBLE BOOKS LLC

NIMBLE BOOKS LLC

Nimble Books LLC

1521 Martha Avenue

Ann Arbor, MI, USA 48103

http://www.NimbleBooks.com

wfz@nimblebooks.com

+1.734-330-2593

Copyright 2013 by Daniel I. Radakovich

Printed in the United States of America

ISBN-13: 978-1-60888-137-6

CONTENTS

INTRODUCTION

The first reaction of the reader may well be—"So what?" What, after all, is the use of studying—or even caring about—the views of a general so patently inept as that Gascon Marshal—that man whose appointment was wholly political, or for the exalting of Napoleon's first fiancée, and not for military ability: that person who—according to the overwhelmingly Bonapartist histories comprising English-language Napoleonic scholarship—was foolish, sly, treacherous, treasonous, always late and probably on purpose!—and who was no good even when he did appear ... et cetera, ad nauseam, ad infinitum. For, given the present bent of writers in this tongue, readers with any familiarity with the period have well-known: Bernadotte the timorous at Austerlitz (cf. de Ségur), Bernadotte the dastard at—or rather, NOT at—Jena/Aüerstadt, Bernadotte the fathead who was at—or rather, NOT at—Eylau, Bernadotte the bungler and boaster who was relieved "*sur-le-champ*" at Wagram (per Marbot), Bernadotte the dragged-screaming-and-kicking-by-Londonderry-to-Leipzig (per Londonderry, aka Sir Charles Stewart).

These, all these, the Napoleonic aficionado must have met ... yet these, all these, are purest fiction, stuff of no more (and yet no less) than any other fabled characters in old morality plays and bogeyman tales. Were they true, still there would be reason to study his maxims, principles, and actions (and/or inactions) to learn, were it but as cautionary admonishments how to act best by doing the opposite!

Alas, however, this poor justification does not exist, for that "traitorous marshal" of Napoleonic legend and whole-cloth fabrication, that boob who according to Thiers' cockeyed *weltanschaaung* "never led above 20,000 men, and then always as a subordinate and never a commander- -in-chief, until he got command of the Army of Northern Germany in 1813" (despite clear, hard evidence to the contrary!); this man—hah! dare one call so wretched a creature a *man?*—this THING, then, that led a reader of *Empires, Eagles, and Lions Review* to plaintively inquire: "considering his ill-behavior everywhere, why did Napoleon make him a marshal?" [this is actually drastically toned-down from his words, to be found in EEL # 102, pp.52-3]—this *being phantastical* shall not be encountered here. Here, perhaps for the first time for most readers, are presented some excerpts of the thought and guiding principles of the man who eventually would freely be elected king of a foreign country by no striving or politicking of his own; one (admittedly self-confessed) of the First Captains of his era, the general whose men never lost a battle—a record only a certain British Duke could match; the hero of Saint-Quentin, Fleurus, Maastricht, Mannheim, Teining, the Tagliamento, the storrn of Gradisca, the repulse of the Quiberon Bay expedition and the taming of the Chouans and the Vendée; the decisive factor at Austerlitz, Jéna *and* Aüerstadt *both* though he knew it not; the destroyer of his enemy at Halle and Lübeck; the thrasher of Bennigsen at Mohrungen; the retainer of bridgeheads at Spanden and Linz; the savior of the arrny at Wagram; the preserver of Antwerp a là Belisarius; and—on the *Coalition* side—the *eminence grise* of the Russian campaign; the architect of Grossbeeren, Dennewitz, and the Trachenberg Plan and of the manoeuvre of Düiben; the decider of Leipzig; and the victor at Ratzeburg and Fridriksthal.

Here shall be seen Bernadotte as Churchillian sustainer of the young Revolution during his tenure as Ministre de Guerre during ten short weeks in 1799, the consummate diplomat who orchestrated the 4th Coalition against its usurper in 1812-3, the man who was loved not alone by political, social, and cultural leaders of France, but like Lafayette, wore the titles of "Father and Friend" of the Revolution until late in 1813, when Napoleon finally dared tell his 'big lies"; who was still loved even by the people over whom he was set as a stranger or even an enemy; who practically single-handedly raised Germany to counter-balance France, and was so beloved by his old troops that they deserted to him on the field of battle in the heat of combat!

The following *maxims* were taken from a pamphlet written by Bernadette's grandson (himself a King of Sweden), as neither Bernadotte nor his son Oscar seem to have left any actual testament of the ex-marshal's views. However, they are so reflective of the remarks that may be culled from other sources, that they appear to be a direct compilation of years of distilled thought garnered from close proximity with the Gascon paterfamilias, or derived from that training given by schools and by an army wholly remade in his image.

This was written in the later era of the needle gun and breech-loading cannon, and specific commentary regarding those technologies is elided; what was retained pertains either to universal principles of warfare or specifically to troops, equipment, and training in the Napoleonic era.

It also must be recalled that Carl XV was the grandson of Napoleon's adopted son Eugene Rose de Beauharnais. Carl's full name was Charles (after his grandfather and adoptive great-grandfather, Carl-Johan and Carl XIII) Louis (after his great-uncle Louis I of Bavaria, who had served under Bernadotte in Bohemia in 1805) Eugene (after his maternal grandfather the former Viceroy of Italy, Prince of Eichstadt and Duke of Leuchtenberg—at least Carl escaped the "Rose"). So it is also possible some of the following comments came from the distaff side, as well as possibly being from his later instructors and of course his own inspiration and whatever genius he himself may have had for studying war. Many forget that although Sweden remained at peace in his reign as it had in his father's and grandfather's time, it was a steadily armed and wary cold war sort of peace, nearing conflict several times(particularly during the Crimean War and Austro-Prussian/Danish wars). The methodology of selection was restricted to those principles and maxims which seem more universal or oriented to comments likely made for earlier times.

NIMBLE BOOKS LLC

GENERAL PRINCIPLES

1) Form a small, but good, army sooner than a large army in which the core will be too mixed with inexperienced soldiers. A good disposition in the spirit of the army is the presage of victory. A healthy diet and suitable clothing contribute here.

It is known that Bernadotte preferred the size of his personal corps to be as homogenous and nimble as he could make it, refusing added auxiliary divisions in 1806 and 1807, culling his field regiments to two battalions or squadrons in preference to three, or one in preference to two battalions if the amount of physical bodies or competent leadership was not there to justify it. If during the campaign depot tactical units came up and the main units had not suffered too much attrition, he would sometimes allow a third unit provided it could catch up. Note this refers to the operational size of the army or corps, not the tactical size of units. He was also well-known for his attention to the creature comforts of the soldier, probably relict from his service as a sergeant in the old French Royal Army.

2) It is necessary that the position of the troops be such, that they know themselves free and unconstrained in their movements. All force kills contentment.

This refers to the practice of practically imprisoning soldiers as the Prussians did in cantonments/garrisons.

3) Combination [of strategy, operations, tactics, and the various troop-types] is indispensable, as much as accumulation [mere

7

weight of numbers either initially or piece-meal] is undesirable. The first gives force, the second produces confusion.

This is why a trained boxer beats a heavier brawler if he is without skill.

4) *At the start of a campaign, make no manuevers that will later be forced to recoil without combat.*

This means to avoid the demoralizing effect of moving without something to show for it.

5) *With an insufficiently-exercised force, avoid battle, seek to train your troops in some small engagements: but, in these, take the offensive.*

Cf. Lückau in 1813.

6) *The more an army lacks in force (i.e. strength), the more it has need of agility, and the more it must hold itself to the offensive.*

The first part sounds very Bernadottesque, but the second does not, even in his French phase, for he is known for having argued with Napoleon that the defensive strategic position was to be preferred, and often refused to undertake offensive missions with what he felt were insufficient means ... Italy in 1797, 1799, on the Rhine in 1799, into Sweden from Zeeland in 1807-9, into Bohemia in 1809, Catalonia in 1809, and in spring in 1813 in Northern Germany. The second part does, however, correspond to Swedish doctrine of the era, a relict from Carl XII's headlong charge methods.

7) *We rarely suppose someone attacking is less numerous; in any case, we must believe them well-supported.*

This prudent assumption is in keeping with Bernadotte's actions at Teining, Möhrungen, Linz, and elsewhere, in the tactical and operational spheres. This is a justification for the comment before it about the offensive being suitable for a small force.

8) *You should never imagine that the enemy might manuever badly or lack courage. That presumption engenders defeat.*

Bernadotte's art of war is directed inwards, with the aim of correctly positioning one's own assumptions about the opponent.

9) *Anyhow, look to the offensive, when that can be done; it is already being half victorious. If, the day of combat taking place, the leader finds himself irresolute, let him attack first.*

This refers mainly to tactical action.

10) *Unite your forces, but do not accumulate them. [In short, have then supporting each other but not clumped together] Flank attacks will then be of less value [against you]*

Bernadotte's old subordinate D'Erlon did NOT obey this at Waterloo in his initial phase of march on that day.

11) *Fear not an enemy of the same force as you, even if his wings surpass your own. Stretched-out arms leave [a fighter's]) chest unprotected.*

Here Bernadotte demonstrates an admirable mastery of basic analytic geometry if two equivalent forces are spread over differing areas, the force that is spread over the larger area must be less concentrated.

12) *Never fight in a single line. That is like the gamester hazarding all on one card.*

That is, have some reserves. France would have been wise to hark back to Bernadotte's wisdom when, in May 1940, the risky gamble of throwing all their mobile reserves and the BEF into the Dyle River plan made both these last two observations pertinent.

13) *Avoid placing the reserve immediately behind the divisions which are found under fire; each ball which passes over the first lines risks striking them. A corps inactive, yet still exposed to enemy fire, is easily discouraged.*

Bernadotte is one of the few Napoleonic era generals who, like Wellington, regularly chose a reverse slope for men awaiting combat, allowing them to *"aisez-vos-jambes"*—sit or lay down until needed. This practice was to cause some confusion at Gross-Beeren as it was alien to Russian and Austrian tactics which preferred a forward slope deployment. Stationing the reserve on the reverse slope required good confidence in the skirmish line and artillery placed on the front slope.

Bernadotte's thinking here was quite modern in that it echoes the financial practice of diversification, which fails if the diversified assets are not actually independent. There is no point to putting a reserve in a place where the failure of the main body may also cause the reserve to fail.

14) *Do not fatigue the men before the combat.*

A chief concern of Bernadotte's always.

15) *Look to animate and exalt the soldiers in taking them to the attack; enthusiasm increases courage.*

This was one of Bernadotte's chief strong points, acknowledged by all. He was known also for rallying men, and earned the sobriquet *Jupiter stator des mutins*—Jupiter standing amongst the mutineers—for his daring rescue of his colleague Marceau from a band of mutineers who were about to kill him. His belief in inspirational leadership was unusual among leaders of the period, most of whom who were professionals and expected their trained troops to be so too. Even those who did indulge in spectacular grandiosity, like Napoleon, disdained it in subsequent commentaries at St. Helena as only useful with partly-trained troops.

16) Never trust in the exclusive effect of fire to leave a combat victoriously. Begin these with fire, [yet] it is only with cold steel ["1 "arme blanche"] that the true fruits of victory may be gathered.

Loosely, don't rely on a cannonade to do much. This is akin to the theory of Dr. Paddy Griffith that the chief cause of tactical British success was not the "line vs. column" concept pushed by Oman and Fortescue, but from the British line holding its fire for maximum effect then charging at enemies after they had been attritted by artillery and skirmisher fire and then by the main volley. (Griffith 1997). This precept was borne out by Bernadotte's experience that throughout the campaign of 1813 Swedish cannonades only had any salutary effect when carried out with combination with Biilow's and Langeron's physical attacks. .

17) Manuever your men as little as possible against the enemy men advancing; as those who return to a combat always cede place to those who throw themselves there.

In short, don't outsmart yourself by feigning abandonment of a position then attempting to retake it.

18) Give blow for blow, without which things will turn to your disadvantage.

Don't be static in combat where things are only done to, and nothing by, you.

19) When the attack takes place, be prompt and decisive in your movements.

20) When we go to attack, it is necessary to conserve moderation. Precipitation is often followed by panic.

This refers to conserving order and not charging in an undisciplined manner. Bernadotte was always known as one who kept a close hand on his cavalry, when he had any, as was shown on the second day at Wagram where he took charge of the Reserve cavalry due to Nansouty's injuries in addition to the Saxons remaining, supporting Macdonald and Masséna's redeployment(s).

21) Do not give up on a combat as long as the main divisions of the army have not yet been employed. In a balance at equilibrium, the least weight decides the balance.

This refers to tenacity, and the second part to economy of force: cf. 1813 and the operations of the Army of Northern Germany. More mathematical thinking.

22) After a long peace, no sacrifice that can make us victors in the first battle can be too great. Even in supposing that the troops will be fatigued after the combat, pursue as much as possible, as long as victory has crowned their efforts

If you pause to take breath, so will your foe.

This had strong influence on Swedish actions in Spring, 1813, in the loss of Harnburg due to insufficient means to hold it, despite its temptingness.

This, for Bernadottte, could certainly be qualified to mean "as long as it is not so far or disordered an advance that it allows the enemy to recover from the blow you dealt him by a morale-rebuilding blow against your pursuit," for so he acted after Austerlitz, Jena/Auerstaedt, and GrossBeeren, in every case of which had an all-out pursuit *à l'outrance* occurred the results might have been disastrous.

23) Never enterprise attacks with a lot of men: a reduced number, but of choice (troops) is worth most; a great number moves slowly and guards silence less.

This refers to sieges and ambuscades more than formal field attacks.

24) Hold a body (of men) in reserve to reinforce an ambush in its success; but be sure that body has the conviction that we have need of them.

[to be there.]

25) Broken country often slows the enemy, some wood edges, defended stubbornly, will generally make him believe that a great force is hidden there.

26) For the defense of villages, of abatis of trees, etc. it will often be better -not to occupy, with the principal force, the point that one must defend.

Cf. Teining, where Bernadotte defended a village and advanced to where he absolutely had to be defeated before the objective could be seized.

27) In this situation, employ a considerable part of forces upon the flank[s] , to go to encounter those that take it up, or for attacking the flank of those who attack [it] .

28) By this method, the principal position, once occupied, should not be allowed to be abandoned. Because it is to these troops, placed on the flank, who alone should pursue.

Bernadotte was concerned that the forces in a principal position should not recklessly advance out of it, and then fall prey to a flanking manuever, counter-attack, or pursuit. Bernadotte had an overriding concern with order. He also wanted to ensure that pursuits did not become disordered by intermixing troops from the flank with those from the principal position, whether it was the flanking force or the main line, as at Möhrungen, that pursued.

Be generous to prisoners: an adversary vanquished is no longer an enemy. This practice not only won him his crown in large part, but also gave his old troops—who may well have grumbled at this "love thy enemy" stuff at the time—the courage to defect at Leipzig).

30) Give to the soldier the part of fame which is his just due. They are the fingers that make the closed fist .

Bernadotte was the most charismatic of the French Marshals and most beloved by his men in every army: in the French, he won the title of *"Père et ami"*—"Father and Friend"—which only Moreau shared. The Bavarians post-1805 tried ever to gravitate to his side in 1806 and 1809, when some did, at Wagram. For the Saxons' part hey wept when he left in 1809; for the Coalition troops in 1813: "when the Prince enters our camp it is a pleasure, a joy! He is extremely beloved." (Comte Balmaine to Count Lieven, *Wellington's Correspondence* 1813)

31) It is rare that the precipitation, even on campaign, is so great, that the troops have not the time to acquit themselves of their duties to God.

This seems more in tune with the spirit of Carl XV than Carl XIV Johan, though the latter did organize *Te Deums* after Leipzig and Dennewitz.

32) You have well prepared the victory, it is God alone that gives it.

This, though, is something either might say, as it fits Bernadotte's Southern streak of fatalism too.

THE COMMANDER

33) No commander may hope for success with some assurance, if he knows not how to like and honor the troops. Love is the basis for obedience.

Another reason for why it was given. Bernadotte is known to have had recourse twice, however, to capital punishment—once in a mutiny where he shot a ringleader, once at Liibeck where he shot a drunken looter who had threatened himself and his staff as they tried to restore order—he found him as at the time he struck him across the face with his marshal's baton.-though it may well have actually been a riding whip. Yet it was his adherence to the above principle that made such occasions notably rare, so that they did not harm, but rather enhanced, his popularity with the rank and file, who under his command preserved the highest standard of discipline in any contemporary army, procuring diplomatic assets unusual for the time by the very passage of his forces-Prussian South German territories Anspach and Baireuth in1805, Lübeck in 1806, Hanover from 1804 and Hamburg from 1808.

35) Do not tolerate, from your inferiors, any inexactitude in the exercise of their functions; cameraderie will lose nothing by this.

By this is shewn that although subordinates are held strictly to account, they are to be treated with "cameraderie"'—another reason he was popular, and a chief reason why his subordinates were to be found with high and independent commands after leaving him. Bernadotte has the distinction of a third of the Marshals of France active near the time of his death [within 5 years] having been his direct subordinates.—D'Erlon, Maison, Grouchy, Gérard. In the modern era, we give great respect to those who have large "coaching trees" of successful protegés.

35) Develop the particular dispositions of each individual . The more there will be capacities among those who serve beneath you, the more there will be leaves to your crown of Laurels.

For example, strong points, attributes, abilities, rectifications of weaknesses, etc.

36) TO HAVE YOUR MEN IN HAND means to say not only to hold them together so they hear your voice and find themselves under your eyes, but more to be able to conduct them and animate them by the attachment that you have known how to inspire in them.

By these precepts Bernadotte became famous as a rallier of troops known, as mentioned earlier, by the sobriquet of *Jupiter Stator des Matins.*

37) Attribute sooner to chiefs than subordinates the causes of errors they commit.

This is another reason for the popularity Bernadotte enjoyed. His attitude was similar to the naval tradition that a captain bears ultimate responsibility for all that occurs in his command. Note that Bernadotte may have been speaking not just in terms of external behavior, but in terms of inward thought; warning the commander to avoid "scapegoating" in his private thoughts.

38) Do not reprove, in front of subordinates, those who command.

This strengthened discipline; however, its corollary, that subordinates should not reprove commanders before the men, Bernadotte did not always have the fortitude to resist--cf. Wagram on the 6th though there the pressure of the situation and his own fever had much to do with this lapse.

39) Make solemn the encouragements and all recompense; that exalts the sentiment of honor.

40) Do not enter into details too much: it is a fog in which we easily lose ourselves.

"Leave me be, I have a lot more to do than to occupy myself with the details of your artillery. When I commanded French troops, I said 'I wish to make this or that movement' and all arranged itself in consequence"—spoken to Suremain on October 4th 1813. Note, the cited context shows it was probably said with a laugh, but it hurt the old emigré's *amour-propre* all the same, though probably in the least severe way. In such cases, better to avoid comment, but if it must be done, do it amicably as here. Langeron's criticism of overmuch detail in Bernadotte's plan of battle at Leipzig is not a proper litmus test, as it was a complex manuever and unique situation.

42) If the army suffers deprivations, take your share in them; if the soldier has lowered spirits, be cheerful, and cheer him up

See in them the man, feel and think for him.

In this is the secret of Bernadotte. The use of "cheerful" in the translation is a regrettable example of cowardice on the part of the translator for not using the literal and quite valid translation of *"Sois gai, et égaye-le"* due to a morose apprehension of it being taken the wrong way by one of two chuckleheaded minorities—only one of which is the US armed forces. .

43) Never canton your entire army, raise barracks only for a part and alternately lodge there every corps. A cantonment of long duration relaxes and weakens discipline.

By this alternation jealousy is avoided--another reason for high morale in Bernadotte's men.

44) *If a contagious malady appears in part of the army, separate in time that part from the others. It is necessary to necessary to raise camp. The change of air is salubrious, and the troops which stay in place are easily attritted by the contagion.*

Pre-Pasteur medical technique for which is now known the cause of its effectiveness. This has much to show of Bernadotte's psychological makeup, and is the root of the draconian measures taken post-Napoleonic Wars to prevent advent of the cholera epidemics that swept Europe, however to the detriment of its freedom of internal movement and balance of trade.

45) *Do not hobble the men with useless baggage. Superfluity in this engenders slowness and makes them accustoned to inappropriate comforts.*

"facilite aux soldats les raffinements hors de saison", or "facilitates refinements that are out of season" is the actual French text here.

46) *Meanwhile, always look to have several days munitions in reserve.*

47) *Simplify all service of campaign.*

These last few maxims are part of why I Corps was noted for being the hardest-marching corps in the Grande Armée, and why Bernadotte was noted for his achievement of amazing marches throughout his career: it is notable that although Napoleon accused him twice of being too slow to cross rivers when there was no chance of doing so in the time the Emperor had allotted. On one of these occasions Bernadotte was to aid Mortier at Diirrenstein, but at the crossing-point there was no means of passage found and one had to be built from scratch. The other occasion was in 1806 when Bernadotte was ordered to pass the Elbe, and the order given to cross that stream had only been issued by Imperial headquarters two hours before on that same day. It was also the only one (message) making the ridiculous asseverations re any delays by Bernadotte in his arrival at Jena/Auërstadt and the earlier year alleged non-arrival at Mortier's affair at Durrenstein that was used in a typically Napoleonic "false accusation to spur results" manner to try to get a speedy passage of the Elbe River, which due to a series of delayed receipts of dispatches at IHQ had occasioned an Imperial snit-fit tantrum...and which made its engenderer feel pretty ridiculous himself when 'called' upon these false claims in the next return post. By then it was found that a) Bernadotte had already long passed the Elbe at Barby, considerably before he could reasonably have been expected to, and this had occurred *before* the first order to do so had arrived from IHQ [let alone the snit-fit one succeeding it], and b) The true author of both the earlier situations [Jena/Auërstadt and pre-Durrenstein] through his earlier, faultily-transmitted instructions—the chief of staff major-general & Marshal Alexander Berthier—was the uncomfortable intermediary of the crossing messages who apparently quickly worked to defuse the argument. The thin skin of the Imperial personage could not afford the appearance of error, however, so the ending was the ungracious pout of the "empereur is not accustomed" note found in the *Correspondance*. Unfortunately, many subsequent readers have taken that letter out of context, without knowing the I Corps despatch in between, the preceding IHQ orders' confusion before, and the general strategic situation, especially when viewed through post-1812 filters.

48) At the beginning of the campaign, the general should inspect in person the measures taken for the surveillance for the camp. It is by itself of a nature so unattractive [peu attrayante], that, without this, it risks being neglected.

49) Do not only trust what spies say.

I.e., use several sources of intelligence and your brains.

50) Do not put your confidence in a single messenger to carry an important message. It is less difficult to be able to seize one victim rather than two.

Recall the unfortunate event before Eylau for a rather painful reason why this would stick in the marshal's mind. Berthier's courier to I Corps was, intentionally or not, intercepted by Cossacks without an auxiliary method of contact being provided.

51) Make the orders you give be repeated. to be certain you are well understood.

52) Never content yourself with a report that only announces to you that the enemy is in view.

53) Incomplete reports generate worry, but little enlightenment.

54) The report should contain: The vicinity in which the enemy is to be found, what is his force; the type of arm with which he is the best provided; if he is in movement or in repose.

Note-this is the irreducible minimum, and is geared to a long-hand information transfer technology in communications or an oral transfer method after considerable temporal delay through the storage capacity of the human mind alone.

55) Do not slow the march of the army by useless reconnaissances: they cause nothing but indecision, the greatest of all faults.

Compare the battles of Halle, Möhrungen, and Linz where the defeated party made these errors.

56) Hold to the greatest activity each part individually but do not undertake a precipitate movement with the whole; without this [precaution] you will stray from the end [purpose].

This helps explain also why several controversial decisions were made by Bernadotte, such as his failure to commit the whole army to an attack at GrossBeeren, the recall of Skjoldebraend at Dennewitz, and the arrested advance at the foot of the Pratzen at Austerlitz and at the Ilm at Jena and Auerstadt. In each case a desirable end in itself had been reached, and further action was to risk the advantage gained. It is worth noting that in every case the restrained or uncommitted force was outnumbered by over 2:1 by the forces it was facing, none of which had previously routed.

57) While you are in movement, do not make continual halts. March while it is necessary, following that repose yourself.

This refers to strategic and operational marches, not to tactical ones where halts to restore order or to guard against surprise or sudden moves are a hallmark of the Marshal's career. It also does not refer to necessary pauses for essential rest during any march, it is more in the sense of not tamely following a schedule of say six hours march, then a repose, then six hours' march, etc. At Halle, Lübeck, Möhrungen, Linz, and Dennewitz victory for his arms followed grueling marches that allowed victory over his opponents, "taking from him his cannons, his powder, his provisions, and that not only without weakening this army but almost without fatiguing itself; because the prince has the art of giving us repose in extreme and pressing cases"—Balmaine to Lieven, op. cit

58) As soon as as you find yourself in the proximity of the enemy, always be ready to accept combat.

This precaution led to most of the "delays" with which observers qua spies such as the British Sir Charles Stewart (Londonderry) and the émigré Frenchman Pozzo di Borgo (acting for the Russians) had so little patience during the Army of Northern Germany' It is, however, not merely moot as to whether the absence of need for the precautions was not occasioned by having undertaken them in the first place! So too might "sour" grapes have questioned the worth of being so high on the vine before when the fox in Reynaud's fable came by, for after all, he ate them not! And the historians accepting them since are like those taking the word of the fox that their sourness made it a fatuous fear in any case.

59) If you must advance, do so quickly, if you must retire, do so slowly, but do not halt any longer than good order requires.

Note the concern with halting to regain order.

60) If several brigades or divisions march together, and we await a battle, have them go as much as possible in order-of-battle.

61) As [marching in order-of-battle] is fatiguing, make several short marches each day [while in such close proximity]. Celerity is not as essential as cohesion.

Note again the stress on being in order.

62) If the march has to take place along a valley, have the flanking escorts climb the foothills and the summit of the heights.

63) We can then make use of signals in place of the system of reports, which is always fatiguing.

64) Do not detach small corps to great distances; isolated, the links [in the "chain" of advanced posts] no longer form a chain.

This refers to patrols and outposts, not raiding expeditions such as Czernitschew's or Wobeser's in mid-1813 in Northern Germany which destroyed the puppet Kingdom of Westphalia then held by

Napoleon's brother Jerome, though it could be argued that Dö-beln's move onto Hamburg in early 1813 unsupported by anyone also violated this precept as no-one could possibly have succored him there.

65) When it is necessary to pass great rivers, do not be content with a single ford, as long as several exist.

This sheds light on the need for several passages over the Elbe in 1813, which proved so essential, and on the need for the posting of Langeron on the Parthe River's line from Eutritsck to Plaussig at Leipzig on 18 October 1813.

66) If you are uncertain of the enemy's movements, take up a defensive attitude. In halting yourself, never remain in march order.

67) Provisional entrenchments are good for covering an inferior force against a superior, but continually raising them fatigues the soldier, slows movements, and indicates fear.

This comment may reflect the post-Crimean/US Civil War perspective of Carl XV and not Bernadotte's.

68) Avoid battle, when you have a defile behind you.

It is debatable whether this is a proper criticism of the Allied conduct at Waterloo. The forest was directly north of the fight at Mont St. Jean, but the northeastern part of the field had a rather wide gap through with the Anglo-Allied army could have retired either to Homs for reuniting with the corps there or upon Brussels to its north on the road to Antwerp. Note that had the Duke of Brunswick and the King of Prussia not kept the bulk of their forces out of immediate combat in the fighting at Aüerstadt due to fears of a putative, then actual, movement of Bernadotte's and the Reserve cavalry's forces off their southern flank, that fight might well have ended badly for III Corps, which is why it kept prolonging its right flank to be able to retire towards Freiburg rather than back over the Koesen bridge through its defile if repulsed.

69) As soon as the enemy is near and that a combat may take place, your troops should be provisioned, preferably with dried food and coffee. By this means you reserve to yourself the hours others will lose in cooking and you will no longer need much baggage.

70) Beware of false alarms. They prevent a very necessary repose for supporting the fatigues of the next day.

Compare the peregrinations of the Saxon Prinz Johann's Chevaulegers caused by interference from Imperial Headquarters at Wagram on October 5th 1809.

71) Establish as soon as possible a troop apart: augment the ordinary surveillance, for guarantee from attacks.

72) Be sure to reconnoiter well before attacking with vigor. Visible foes mislead easily.

73) Do not give to a regiment or to a battalion all of its munitions. That will lead it to be prodigious with them, and you will have no cartridges in reserve.

74) Cede to a capable cavalry officer, the Direction of that arm upon the battlefield. It is necessary that he be free in his dispositions. Indicate to him only the principal points.

Officers such as Murat [Gradisca], Kellerman [before Munich 1805], Gerard [Linz 1809], Beeieres [Wagram], Nansouty [fall

1806], Skjoldebraend [Bornhoft] and Manteuffel [Leipzig]. played this role for Bernadotte at various times.

75) Tell the general of division or of brigade that if he does not find himself present on the battlefield, he should, in default of orders, direct himself to the side from where the cannonade is to be heard the loudest. The warrior should not avoid, but seek, the combat.

[And, yes, he did do this at Jéna/ Aüerstadt, in 1806, though the story is too long to go into here.]

Thus did Gérard argue with Grouchy in 1815 in a discussion before Wavre—both marshals were previously subordinates of Bernadotte, as was D'Erlon, who was also at Waterloo.

76) Designate to the commander of each considerable detachment the position which, in the limit of his possible action, he should preferably attack and take.

77) Strike with force there where you find an obstinate resistance.

This differs from much other advice, which is to go around resistance. In this case it refers to using the initial probes to determine what is valuable in the enemy's eyes to seize or retain acting upon the principle that if the enemy wants it—take it from him!

78) A chief should see and be seen as well as staying in his place as long as all goes well. He should not expose himself without necessity but as soon as he sees the men falter, he will then take himself to the neighborhood where the fighting is strongest, and there he should be immovable.

Here in the text come several admonitions that at the time the translator felt would be superfluous for the "but" of studying possible Napoleonic-era elements in the discourse.

INFANTRY

Much of this part of the work deals with post-Napoleonic changes in weaponry and tactics, so those principles and maxims have not been here recopied, except when they seem reflected in the Gascon's career. Numeration will stay consistent in text, skipping over sections that have been excluded.

83) In all the infantry, each private must carry two arms[weapons]. If one will not serve, he has recourse to the other. He that, as long as there remains to him one arm/weapon, quits the man-to-man combat, is a coward.

This refers to the need for musket and bayonet.

84) No troop of infantry nor troop of chasseurs [ight infantry] should be composed uniquely of young men or of veterans. Each age has its faults, as well as its [good] qualities.

87) Do not choose young men for skirmishers. "Sang-froid" is rare among the young.

89) Don't believe a soldier [to be] bad, because he is not eager for the chase [i.e. always racing forwards]. He who does not advance fast, will not hasten more to recoil.

In this too can be seen why the marshal was popular. Men are different, although alike. He hereby grants his men room rationalization, whereby someone feeling a momentary as well as a constant reluctance to go towards danger, can retain that self-esteem that prevents yielding to cowardice or succumbing to despair. Few are the bases for self-esteem that cannot be re-established, if only those to re-establish it can be gotten to do so. And they cannot, if they feel themselves to be dirt. Calling people dirt has only a positive—i.e. enraging—effect when the individuals know it is not so—if it is believed, such but reinforces despair and lassitude.

90) Do not believe a chasseur advanced in age is good for nothing. "Sang-froid" and a sure eye can distinguish him, despite his years.

Though this refers to the post-Napoleonic phase of glorification of light infantry notable in the Restoration, Orléanist, and 2nd Empire armies—"Zouaves and all that"—this illustrates what was part of the Marshal's makeup, a strong sensitivity to ageing questions—which led him to have some awful fixes and misunderstandings, to surround himself with youthful staff whereby he partook to himself some of their liveliness so akin to his own *"en campagne"* and which led him to expedients such as commissioning march battalions of "invalid corps" in 1806 during the pursuit of Blücher, in 1809 for the Saxon forces, and for the Army of Northern Germany's forces 1813-4. By these expedients, those not able to physically keep up with the grueling marches would not be subjected to the indignity and shame of being stragglers—and ergo often deserters—but were retained under army discipline and fortified with the knowledge that their presence was still desired and needed by their comrades as soon as they could rejoin, which allowed them that extra spark to get their moves a bit faster, and ameliorated as much as possible the attrition on the march despite seeming at first glance to increase it. For the true malingerers knew that by hanging back, they could gain no shelter from unpleasant tasks, so all but the most recalcitrant gave up the idea—and from these little could be hoped anyway. This also happened tactically. Bernadotte's action in retiring Dupas' decimated French division from the front line at Wagram on the 6th and sending it to Raasdorf where it—and NOT the Saxons—was engaged in rallying and reforming stragglers—NOT of Bernadotte's IX Corps, but of other corps—effectively preserved for *l'Empereur* approximately one thousand men in a state of combat-readiness who otherwise would have been "missing"—not inclusive of those stragglers that they sent back to rejoin still-cohesive units. The remaining Saxon infantry marched around the back of Macdonald's Army of Italy in good order and supported its left flank and the many cavalry actions of the Saxon Corps and the reserve cavalry initially under Nansou, later upon his injury under Bernadotte, between there and Masséna's reforming corps along the Danube.

91) All soldiers should learn to shoot, tactics requires it , and during the fusillade his judgment and his presence of spirit develop themselves.

Bernadotte always relied upon *l'ordre-mince*—lines—for his combats, save at Halle where Dupont's men were sent in in a sort of *ordre-mixte* of alternating columns and lines due to terrain constraints until all the columns could deploy. This is another reason his forces usually suffered low casualties, whenever they fought, and was a key reason he blew up at Napoleon on the second day at Wagram when some officious aide from the imperial headquarters tried to force Bernadotte's Saxons into closed columns while they were at the focal point of an arc of enemy artillery with a crossfire of 270 degrees—supposedly "by the Emperor's express order" which Bernadotte *sur-le-champ* countermanded saying angrily "Deploy, deploy! I am not accustomed to losing men unnecessarily!" This is likely from IHQ's misconception of a Saxon fragility, which was not from ill-training, but from heavy losses the night before. They recently had evolved from the Frederician system which was prepared to accept heavy fire losses in linear formations and had not yet had the experience with raw troops in columns which they were to better employ in 1813-4. The French expected the Saxons to be at their reputed strength of 30,000, which attrition, friction of the campaign, and detachments by IHQ had whittled down to just 8,000 on the 5th for operations. The severe losses the Saxons had suffered in the night's fighting and the morning's cannonade seemed horrifically vast and colored people's impressions, though as Savary—of many memoir writers, the only one actually present—and an enemy of Bernadotte— acknowledged, they held firm when Masséna's men had to withdraw.

95) The intervals between the files should not be determined with too exact minuteness.

Do not waste time on unessential parade-ground niceties. In combat troops too close would jumble and jostle each other from terrain irregularities and time wasted on preserving overly neat lines might let opportunity slip or cause preoccupation in the face of danger.

96) It suffices that the necessary rapport be maintained between them.

If it works, it is ok.

103) If one's [soldiers] are exposed to a fire too distant to change our position in an efficacious manner, it will be necessary to advance the troops a little and show them that the balls fall behind them. We thus can augment their courage.

104) If, on a like occasion, we retire a bit looking for a refuge, the contrary [namely, a decrease in courage] easily arrives.

As seen at Wagram, for the Marshal this guideline was modified by his assessment of how well-disciplined the troops were, and of course whether an advance or retreat appeared likely to be cost-effective or not. The Saxons at Wagram on the 6th did a quite creditable job in their shifting back-and-forth to throw off the Austrian aim and—though some officious aides-de-camp and "Nappycorne-latelies" may have thought it "wavering" when they ordered then to close up—they did so without a decrease in courage.

105) A good infantry reserves its fire until it finds itself at a range close and sure.

106) If an inexperienced troop is constrained to halt itself, without permission to fire, it is necessary that the officers be seen before the ranks .

Provided item 33 above applies. If it does not, instead of the troops feeling "there are the brave officers most exposed so no danger exists"—as the officer might think—or "there are those brass hats who ain't found wherever any danger is"—as the men might think—either view is here useful to the purpose—they might think at best "There are those incompetent chumps getting in the way" or at worst "Oh boy, now's our chance to boogie!"—either of which-to the officers at least, could be rather unpleasant

107) Do not attack in columns. Inform the soldier that the more points of the bayonet there are, the more there are also of trembling enemies.

This led to some of Bernadotte's 1813 contretemps with Bülow, who was an avid convert to the "new" "Prussian Style" of tactics defined by Scharnhorst, which exalted the column as a post-1806 tactical innovation. Bernadotte disapproved of columns if not being used to keep the force together closely—i.e. not in combat—as they caused too many casualties in getting their results. Just because someone wins with one method does not automatically mean it is the best—though it is a good argument for retaining it rather than to occasion the chaos of altering it *en campagne*.

108) March in square if you are exposed to a cavalry attack. To form a square quickly is not a thing easy to do in the heat of action.

It is not impossible, though. So did Bernadotte's protégés act at Aüerstadt —Friant, Gudin, and Morand—though they were indeed at the time under the command of Davout. But so many quasi-scholars of the period quibble and balk at giving the Prince of Ponte-Corvo any credit for Dupont's later actions of Halle and Braunsburg, why not treat the duc d'Aüerstadt sinilarly? The French army was a coherent mass, with interwoven personal relationships abounding … notwithstanding the "schools" born from Napleon's successful campaigns with the Armée d'Italie and Armée d'Allemagne. It is impossible to separate out what came from whom, when, and where, but if any guide is needed the similarity between prior actions should give any needed clues.

CAVALRY

136) The horseman must not rely on his firearm, but he also should not disdain it.

In the Napoleonic wars, especially in small actions, during campaigning, mounted and dismounted fire often came the way of the cavalryman. Cossacks especially often would dismount and snipe at force passing by.

139) The cavalry should not remain ahorse while awaiting orders.

This caused exhaustion and decreased efficiency for man and beast, as well as presenting a clearer, larger target for fire. Bernadotte's forté was the crucial cavalry charge, as at Fleurus where it cleared a wood and village, as at Teining where it blighted Archduke Charles' assault, as in every battle he fought in under the Empire—Halle, Möhriingen, Linr, Wagram—Gérard's charges with the Saxons on the 5th August Raasdorf and with the Guard lancers and Saxon chevaulegers to aid Macdonald on the 6th—and tried to do in 1813 with the Russian horse at night at GrossBeeren, the strike of Skjoldebraend in the centre at Dennewitz later recalled. Worontzow's positioning to seize the enemy trains in that battle, and the glorious time-gaining charges of Manteuffel at Leipzig that occupied the whole III Corps showed Bernadotte had not lost his touch ... these being, along with many of the Prussian general Oppeln's charges, equal to any of Murat's in numbers or results.

ARTILLERY

149) Science should be the basis of the practice [of firing], but the practice should not be dominated by the science.

In short. know the equipment's possibilities and best uses, but do not disdain its use under less-than-optimal occasions. Again, this is a very *selon les circonstances* [depending on the circumstances], practical application. To Napoleon, as seen by his notes on famous artillerists Lloyd and Rogniat, practical application was a guiding principle, and why he usually preferred letting the other side make the first move. *See tome 31, Correspondance de Napoléon 1ier.*

156) Never disperse the effect of the artillery.

Though this is applicable to Bernadotte's actions throughout his career, he was a scion of the Revolutionary period in his willingness to act without insisting on great numbers of cannon. Feeling a few well-directed shots were worth more than a massive cannonade—his pursuit of Blücher—and indeed Halle and Lübeck, were done with but 12 French cannon accompanying all I Corps. His subordinate Von Cardell's surgical strikes at GrossBeeren, Dennewitz, and Leipzig were proof of the efficacy of the "You don't need much if it's done well" nature of Bernadotte's utilization of cannon fire. Economy of force was a hallmark of his operations, shown by his support of the divergent assaults of Caffarelli and Vandamme at Austerlitz and repulse of the Russian Imperial Guard there; his operations on October 14th, 1806 in maneuvering to Apolda between both battles of Jéna and Aüerstadt, and proving the chief factor in the retirement of the Prussians from both fields that day. using just Rivaud's division and his own light horse and Beaumont's dragoons; and his superior handling of inferior numbers to achieve local superiorities at critical points at Halle, Möhrunge, Linz, and on August5th at Wagram where with 7,030 men and 2 cannon he did marvels—though it must be admitted one of his divisions wound up getting the Imperial Guard's artillery support by mistake rather than the key one for the assault that night. His economy of force s was a trait which amazed the Coalition officers observing his Army of northern Germany's 1813 actions, like Graf Hammerstein and Count Balmaine who had served under some of the best their side had had to offer in prior campaigns, It also is notable that he always assured himself of superior artillerists. From D'Éblé and Sénarmont through Suremain and Von Cardell, no better gunners in any corps in any army existed. And he generally gave them objectives and then got out of their way, letting them arrange their movements, placements, fire without undue interference.

158) In firing, do so with exactitude, even at the cost of speed, and not vice-versa.

Note this is a maxim for artillery, and not foot musketry, which during the period before breechloading rifles relied more on the morale effect of the volley than the deadliness of the shots, Austrian foot getting a mere 7 rounds/year to practice with just before the 1866 Six-Weeks-War with Prussia.

159) The last blow is the best.

This is like getting the last word in an argument, it is a morale booster and disorders the foe if before a clash it suffers the last bit of damage.

THE GENERAL STAFF

184) He [an aide-de-camp] should destroy in time written letters and orders so that they cannot pass into enemy hands.

This is a relict from the problem that Napoleon's forces encountered with stolen dispatches before Eylau, which may actually have been an IHQ strategem rather than an unintended bungling.

Here ends this work, with a total of 185 items. The bulk of the comments on the General Staff are nothing particularly useful for the historical period concerned for this overview, largely dealing with later developments.

The entirety of the comments by Karl XV can be viewed in a small pamphlet entitled *Resume des Principes Militaires,* J. Dumaine imprimur. Paris, 1872, "extracted from the "Journal des Sciences Militaires" printed in Stockholm in 1866.

AFTERWORD

This, then is at least as good an exercise into the mind of Bernadotte as the soi-disant *"Maxims"* of Napoleon, which has nought save some collated bits of his renarks on Rogniat and Lloyd on St. Helena and bits of the *Correspondance*—nay, better, for those were often taken out of context and had been written to different purposes to divers recipient readers, whilst the lessons received by Carl XV were learnt throughout his life at his grandfather's and his father's knees (for Oskar had learnt, mainly orally, from his father for even longer) when he could question and verify their meanings. What exists in these remarks even if not of the ex-Marshal's origin are bound to be continuations and extrapolations of his thought, and altered far less at the hands of his descendants than Napoleon's work at the hands of alien editors. The comments in small type below the items are this translator's, for which he accepts full responsibility for any error that might occur, relying on his own long study of the Marshal and his career for his confidence that they are apropos. Perhaps in the Royal Archives in Stockholm there may be something better but until such is unearthed this is the best we have.

This work, and some others by Carl XV, had some influence upon French military thought in the post-Crimean era up until WWI. Their stress on the offensive and morale was consistent with the (ultimately disastrous) trends of that era's French thought. Two earlier works by Carl XV had appeared, one on infantry in the post-musket era and one on "modern tactics" which also had some readership. Copies of these ostensibly may be found in Yale's Sealy-Mudd Library, and the pamphlet from which the above was taken this author/translator could only find at the Bibliothèque Nationale de Paris—frenetically hand-copied on the last day of a research trip—so there too some minor error may've crept in, but surely not material in the context of the whole.

If the translator were required to seize upon a single part to explain the appeal of Bernadotte, it would have to be in item 142's "See in the soldier, the Man. Think and feel for him."

BIBLIOGRAPHY

Besides the above-mentioned pamphlet, items 30, 57, and 156 refer to letters found in *Wellington's Supplementary Despatches* vol. viii written by Graf Hammerstein and Comte de Balmaine. Item 40 is found in the *Mémoires du Général de Su remain* by Suremain, item 47 is found in the *Service historique Armée de terre* section of the Archives de guerre, Vincennes. Paris and Langeron's comments on Bernadotte's battle plans for the 18th at Leipzig are from his own *Mémoirs du comte Langeron.* Anecdotal citations are largely from biographical sources too numerous to mention, but the "Pere et ami" bit though mentioned in several appears to be first from the work by Sarrazin, *Histoire du guerre entre Angleterre et France,* which is not to be confused with Londonderry's *Narrative of the late War in Germany and France* alluded to in item #58, nor with Sir Henry Bunbury's *Narrative of the Great War with France*, which has nothing to do with this piece but has a swell account of the Battle of Maida in Italy in 1806 between Reynier and Sir John Stuart that proves the French under Reynier as well as the British fought there in lines, not columns, which reinforces some of the comments herein about Bernadotte's preference for lines. So it gets a plug here too.